Comic-Strip Grammar

40 Reproducible Cartoons With Engaging Practice Exercises That Make Learning Grammar Fun

by Dan Greenberg

SCHOLASTIC
PROFESSIONAL BOOKS

New York • Toronto • London • Auckland • Sydney

Mexico City • New Delhi • Hong Kong

To my parents, my biggest fans.
Also to Simon, Molly, and Leah.

Cover design by Jaime Lucero
Interior design by Jaime Lucero and Kelli Thompson
Cover and interior illustrations by Jared Lee

ISBN 0-439-08681-7
Copyright © 2000 by Dan Greenberg.

TABLE OF CONTENTS

TABLE OF CONTENTS

TOPICS CHART I

Use these charts to select reproducible pages that will fit the individual needs of each student in your class.

TOPICS CHART II

About This Book

For generations, grammar has been a topic that has struck fear in the hearts of both students and teachers alike—not because it isn't necessary or useful, but because it can get so tedious and dull. No longer! *Comic-Strip Grammar* treads where few books have gone before, daring to make grammar both amusing and accessible. Watch your students' faces light up when you give them a page from this book. *Comic-Strip Grammar* really is fun!

Using the familiar characters from *Comic-Strip Math* and *Comic-Strip Story Problems*, the cartoons on these pages use humor and narrative to give students practice in a range of critical grammar topics that are specified by national language arts standards. Topics cover parts of speech, sentence structure, using punctuation, and verb usage, as well as specialty topics such as the use of *lie* and *lay* and *good* and *well*.

Special emphasis is placed on such topics as capitalization, subject-verb agreement, using commas, run-on sentences and fragments, pronouns, possessives, apostrophe use, and comparatives and superlatives. These topics are covered in more than one lesson, so that you may introduce students to key concepts, and then help them to use those concepts in a more complex way.

Using This Book

The book is arranged in five sections: Parts of Speech, Sentences, Using Punctuation, Using Verbs, and Special Topics. Use the Topics Charts to find the particular topic that you are looking for.

Lessons are organized as follows: Each cartoon presents a key concept from the lesson in a humorous context. The final panel of the cartoon provides definitions and examples of concepts that will be used below. Exercises are presented simply at first, with the degree of difficulty increasing toward the bottom of the page.

Complete answers for the exercises are provided on pages 61–64.

In the classroom, the cartoons can be employed in a variety of ways, including:

- whole-class participation—working through the problems together;
- small-group participation—allowing students to find solutions on their own;
- individual participation—assigning pages as classwork, homework, or self-paced study.

Moving On

In addition to showing students that the necessary and often neglected subject of grammar can be fun, I hope that this book conveys the idea that grammar is a powerful tool. By following the conventions of grammar and choosing their words carefully, students not only improve basic communication, but also gain an appreciation for language.

Part 1:
PARTS OF SPEECH

THE BEACH featuring Molly and Rowena

I really love the beach.

Me, too. That reminds me: What did the wave say to the sand?

What are ya DUNE tonight?

Good. Now try this one: What did the sand say back to the wave?

I'm not SHORE. Every time I meet with you I seem to get wet!

Very nice!

YOU ANSWER IT!

Adverbs modify verbs and adjectives. Can you find any adverbs in this cartoon?

(see page 18)

Name: _____

HEART-SHAPED POOL featuring Rowena and Ant Betty

YOU ANSWER IT!

Rowena may not know much about swimming, but when it comes to nouns, she's right up there with the best! How many nouns can you find in this cartoon?

GRAMMAR WORKSHOP

What is a noun? *A noun is a word that names a person, place, thing, or idea.*

People: woman, lawyer, Alex, actor, Cindy, zookeeper, mayor

Places: St. Louis, school, forest, bedroom, Mt. Hood, theater

Things: shoe, magazine, pizza, crayon, broom, soccer ball, brick

Ideas and Feelings: happiness, talent, law, hope, fear, truth

---

Find the nouns in each sentence. Circle the people (or animals). Underline the places. Draw a box around the things. Double-underline the ideas and feelings.

1. Rowena was having a big party to celebrate the grand opening of her swimming pool.

2. Before the party, Ant Betty shopped at Insect World for a new swimming suit.

3. Ant Betty settled on a three-piece model with pink polka dots.

4. A beetle named Mavis arrived at the party wearing the exact same polka-dot suit that Ant Betty had bought.

5. This was a huge shock and an embarrassment to Ant Betty.

6. For a while, Ant Betty stayed in her chair and sipped iced tea with lemon.

7. "Why let such a silly thing ruin your day?" Rowena said.

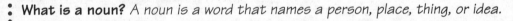

Name: _____

FIX YOUR WAGON featuring Squirmy and Ant Betty

YOU ANSWER IT!

Take action! Help rescue Molly. Then find all the verbs in the cartoon above.

GRAMMAR WORKSHOP

· · · · · · · · · · · · · · ·

What is a verb? A verb is a word that shows action or indicates a state of being. Some verbs are helping verbs that go along with other verbs.

Action verb:
The wagon <u>flipped</u> over.

Mental action:
Molly <u>worried</u> all day.

Verb of being:
Squirmy <u>was</u> tired.

Helping verb:
Molly <u>must</u> escape.

Circle the verb in each sentence. On the line provided, identify each verb as an action verb or a verb of being.

1. Molly and Ant Betty planned a ride to town. _____

2. On the way, just outside of town,

   the road curved sharply. _____

3. Molly and Ant Betty spilled over. _____

4. "Yow!" Ant Betty cried. _____

5. No one was hurt. _____

Write a verb in the space to complete each sentence.

6. After the wagon crash, Squirmy _____ into town to

   get supplies.

7. At the store, Squirmy _____ bandages and

   peanut butter sandwiches.

8. Squirmy _____ back to see how Molly was.

11

Name: _____

NOT YOUR CHEESE featuring Molly and Rudy

YOU ANSWER IT!

Can you find all the pronouns in this cartoon?

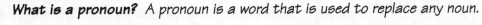

GRAMMAR WORKSHOP

What is a pronoun? A pronoun is a word that is used to replace any noun.

Noun: <u>Molly</u> ate <u>cheese</u>.

Nouns: Did <u>Rudy</u> bring <u>snacks</u> for lunch?

Nouns: <u>Rudy</u> lost the <u>directions</u>.

Pronoun: <u>She</u> ate <u>it</u>.

Pronouns: <u>Who</u> brought <u>them</u> for lunch?

Pronouns: <u>He</u> lost <u>them</u>.

Circle each pronoun.

1. Rudy bought two kinds of cheese from Hal and Sal's Cheese Shop and brought them home.

2. Hal and Sal said they were delicious.

3. Nobody likes cheese more than Molly.

4. "This is good cheese," said Rudy.

5. "I haven't eaten cheese this good since I was a young bunny," Rudy said.

6. "Did you get any Swiss cheese?" Molly asked Rudy.

7. "They didn't have Swiss cheese," Rudy said.

8. "Instead, I got this," Rudy said, pointing to a chunk of moon cheese.

9. "Everyone in the store said moon cheese was delicious," Rudy said.

Name: _____

SICK TREE featuring Dr. Woovis, Moovis, and Judy

YOU ANSWER IT!

Dr. Woovis is a brilliant doctor, but he has made a mistake using a personal pronoun. Can you find it?

GRAMMAR WORKSHOP

What are personal pro-nouns? Personal pronouns replace nouns that refer to the one speaking, spoken to, or spoken about.

These personal pronouns can be used as subjects.

Singular: I, you, he, she, it
Plural: we, you, they

These pronouns are used as objects.

Singular: me, you, him, her, it
Plural: us, you, them

Circle the correct personal pronoun.

1. Dr. Woovis is not like the rest of (we/us).

2. (He/Him) and his sister Woovena studied for years at the famous Dog Medical Academy.

3. (They/Them) learned how to sniff out any dog disease.

4. "(She and me/She and I) love practicing medicine," Dr. Woovis said.

5. Dr. Woovis added, "Helping others is very important to (me/I)."

Each sentence has an error using a personal pronoun. Cross out the incorrect personal pronoun. Write the correct pronoun on the line.

6. "Squirmy and me both felt funny," said Judy.

7. "Dr. Woovis gave medicine to Squirmy and I ," she added.

8. "She and me felt better right away," Squirmy said.

9. Squirmy added, "Us worms think Doc Woovis is tops!"

Name: _____

GEOGRAPHY TIME featuring Squirmy and Woovis

YOU ANSWER IT!

Woovis may know about the world, but he doesn't know about indefinite pronouns. Can you find the mistake he made with an indefinite pronoun?

GRAMMAR WORKSHOP

What are indefinite pronouns? *Indefinite pronouns do not refer to a specific noun.*

Singular *indefinite pronouns include: one, each, anyone, everybody, somebody, nobody, nothing, no one, either, neither, and someone.*

• *Someone* <u>is</u> *home. (Someone is singular)*

Plural *indefinite pronouns include: both, few, many, and several. All, any, most, none, and some can be singular or plural.*

• *A few of the cats were friendly. (few is plural)*
• *All of the cats are home. (all is plural)*
• *All of the cat food is gone. (all is singular)*

Underline each indefinite pronoun. Circle the correct form of each verb in the parentheses.

1. Many of the things that Squirmy says (is/are) ridiculous.

2. No one (say/says) funnier things than Squirmy.

3. Most of Squirmy's sayings (is/are) famous among worms.

4. "Nothing (is/are) lower than a worm," Squirmy once said.

5. One of Squirmy's sayings (was/were) included in the Worm Encyclopedia.

6. Some of the students at Worm University (study/studies) Squirmy's sayings.

Name: _____

DUCK SOUP featuring Woovis and Squirmy

YOU ANSWER IT!

Squirmy used an adjective to describe the soup. Can you find it?

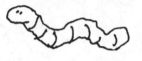

GRAMMAR WORKSHOP

What is an adjective? An adjective is a word that modifies a noun or pronoun.

One adjective: <u>hot</u> soup

Two adjectives: <u>hot</u>, <u>delicious</u> soup

Three adjectives: <u>hot</u>, <u>delicious</u>, <u>noodle</u> soup

Four adjectives: <u>Hot</u>, <u>delicious</u>, <u>noodle</u> soup is <u>good</u> for you.

Underline each adjective in the sentences below.

1. It was a dark and stormy night.
2. Strange smells came wafting up out of the back room.
3. Woovis was in there, making his famous green soup.
4. This horrid soup tastes worse than it smells.
5. The disgusting ingredients give the soup its sickening flavor.

Write the noun that each underlined adjective modifies in the space provided. Circle all other adjectives.

6. Woovis poured the foul soup down the <u>kitchen</u> sink. _____
7. Then Squirmy made a quick call to Soupie's <u>All-Night</u> Soup Shop. _____
8. Squirmy ordered a full pint of <u>black</u> bean soup. _____

Name: _____

ANIMAL JEOPARDY featuring Judy and Chuck

YOU ANSWER IT!

Chuck is not too good at animal facts, but he does use adjectives well. Can you find the adjectives that Chuck uses?

GRAMMAR WORKSHOP

How do you use adjectives? Adjectives are words that modify nouns or pronouns. Take a look at these examples to see how adjectives work.

Sentence: The chef made lunch.
Add Adjectives: The <u>talented</u>, <u>French</u> chef made a <u>fabulous</u>, <u>six-course</u> lunch.
Sentence: The boy ate a meatball.
Add Adjectives: The <u>tall</u>, <u>hungry</u> boy ate a <u>spoiled</u>, <u>green</u> meatball.

Rewrite each sentence. Add adjectives to make each sentence colorful and interesting.

1. The frog asked a question.

_____

2. The mantis gave an answer.

_____

3. The audience clapped its hands.

_____

4. The mantis became a star.

_____

Name: _____

MOON FOOD featuring Judy the Frog and Chuck Mantis

YOU ANSWER IT!

Chuck used an adverb to describe when he ate at the restaurant. Can you find it?

GRAMMAR WORKSHOP

• • • • • • • • • • • • • • • • • •

What is an adverb? An adverb is a word that modifies a verb, an adjective, or another adverb.

Adverb: Chuck stood <u>stiffly</u>.
Adverb: Judy <u>carefully</u> walked past.
Adverb: Chuck was <u>very</u> tired.
Adverb: Judy stopped <u>suddenly</u>.

Circle the adverbs in each sentence.

1. Chuck quietly entered The Moon Dog Café.

2. The waiter floated casually over to Chuck's table.

3. "May I take your order?" the waiter asked politely.

4. "I'll have the moon pie," Chuck said. "I want it cooked thoroughly."

5. "Excellent!" the waiter said. "You've made a very good choice, sir."

Circle one adverb in each sentence. Write the word that the adverb modifies.

6. Chuck ate his moon pie slowly.

7. Meanwhile, Chuck's table gradually rose off the floor.

8. "Help!" Chuck cried frantically. "I'm floating away!"

9. "We're terribly sorry, sir," the waiter said.

Name: _____

THE BEACH featuring Molly and Rowena

I really love the beach.

Me, too. That reminds me: What did the wave say to the sand?

What are ya DUNE tonight?

Good. Now try this one: What did the sand say back to the wave?

I'm not SHORE. Every time I meet with you I seem to get wet!

Very nice!

YOU ANSWER IT!

Adverbs modify verbs and adjectives. Can you find any adverbs in this cartoon?

GRAMMAR WORKSHOP

How do you use adverbs? Adverbs are words that modify verbs, adjectives, or another adverb. Take a look at these examples to see how adverbs work.

Sentence: The pig ran.
Add Adverb: The pig ran <u>quickly</u>.
Sentence: The mouse crossed the big room.
Add Adverbs: The mouse <u>silently</u> crossed the <u>very</u> big room.

Write an adverb in each blank space.

1. The pig basked _____ in the hot summer sun.

2. Waves _____ rolled in on the beach.

3. In the distance, seagulls squawked _____ .

4. "This is the life," the pig said _____.

5. A figure on a surfboard _____ sailed into view.

6. "I _____ wish that I could try that," said the pig.

7. The next day, the pig _____ returned to the beach.

8. The pig _____ paddled out on a wave.

9. The pig _____ rode the wave to the shore.

10. "I'm a real surfing pig!" the pig announced _____.

Name: _____

TRASH TIME featuring Moovis and Woovis

Fump!.

TRASH

Why did you throw your wristwatch into the garbage can?

TRASH

Because I'm wasting time.

Oh.

YOU ANSWER IT!

Misusing time is always a mistake.

So is misusing a preposition

Can you find the preposi-

tion in this cartoon?

GRAMMAR WORKSHOP

What is a preposition? A preposition shows the relationship of a noun or pronoun to some other word in a sentence. A prepositional phrase includes the preposition and its object.

Preposition: Woovis waited <u>for</u> 5 o'clock

Preposition: The watch <u>with</u> the gold band is broken.

Preposition: The time <u>on</u> my watch is wrong.

Prepositional Phrase: Moovis threw the watch <u>out the window</u>.

Underline the preposition in each sentence.

1. Woovis bought a new watch at Widby's Time Shop.

2. The watch cost $29.95 and came with a lifetime guarantee.

3. Woovis gave Moovis the watch for her birthday.

4. The watch came inside a fancy box.

5. Moovis put the watch on her wrist.

6. "This is the best day of my life," Moovis said.

Circle the preposition in each sentence. Underline the entire prepositional phrase.

7. Then one day Moovis took the watch into the swimming pool.

8. The label on the watchband said that the watch was waterproof.

9. Soon, the watchcase filled with water.

Review Section 1

Circle each noun and draw a box around the verb in each sentence. Double-circle each pronoun.

1. My name is Woovis the dog.

2. I am a <u>smart</u> dog.

3. We welcome you to our <u>first</u> review page.

4. We wanted to make this a <u>special</u> review page.

5. This review page contains more than just <u>good</u> problems.

6. It <u>also</u> contains the story of a dog named Woovis.

7. Woovis came to the city from a <u>small</u> farm in the country.

8. His mother <u>often</u> said Woovis was good at grammar.

9. In school Woovis was a <u>top</u> grammar student.

10. The teachers <u>always</u> gave Woovis excellent marks in grammar.

11. Dogs bark <u>loudly</u> when they speak.

12. Woovis speaks <u>many</u> different languages including English and dog-speak.

In sentences 1 to 12 above, identify each underlined word as an adjective or adverb. Choose the correct verb for each sentence below.

13. My friend Squirmy and I (was/were) interested in grammar.

14. Most of my friends (is/are) not dogs.

15. One of my goals (was/were) to appear in a book.

16. Few grammar books (has/have) dogs or worms in them.

Write an adjective or adverb in each space. Then circle each preposition. Underline the entire prepositional phrase.

17. Woovis came from a _____ town in the country.

18. Squirmy _____ waited for years.

19. Woovis and Squirmy appeared in several _____ magazines.

Part 2:

SENTENCES

BANK ROBBERY featuring Squirmy and Woovis

YOU ANSWER IT!

Squirmy's ideas about robbers may be a bit strange, but at least he doesn't have problems with subject and verb agreement. Can you find the mistake that Woovis made? (see page 29)

Name: _____

TREE KNOWLEDGE featuring Woovis and Monica

YOU ANSWER IT!

Woovis may be no expert on trees but he can find four kinds of sentences in this cartoon. Can you?

GRAMMAR WORKSHOP

What are the four kinds of sentences?

A **declarative sentence** makes a statement and ends with a period.
An **interrogative sentence** asks a question and ends with a question mark.
An **imperative sentence** gives a command and ends with a period.
An **exclamatory sentence** shows excitement or strong emotion and ends with an exclamation point.

Identify each sentence as declarative, interrogative, imperative, or exclamatory. Then place a period, question mark, or exclamation point at the end of each sentence.

1. Why should bears know more about trees than dogs _____

2. Bears climb trees more often than dogs _____

3. Give me one good reason why dogs should know about trees _____

4. It's unbelievable — that dog has climbed up a tree _____

5. Actually, the dog was placed in the tree by a fireman _____

6. Both dogs and bears seem to know a lot about trash _____

7. Show me a dog who is not a scavenger _____

8. Look out, there's a bear in that tent _____

Name: _____

CAMP WALLA WALLA BING BANG featuring Woovis and Rudy

YOU ANSWER IT!

The subject of mosquitoes interests Rudy. Can you find a sentence above that has mosquitoes as its subject?

GRAMMAR WORKSHOP

• • • • • • • • • • • • • •

What is a subject? The subject is the person, place, thing, or idea that the sentence tells about.

Sentence: Camp starts today.

Subject: Camp
Sentence tells about: when camp starts

Sentence: Only Rudy knows the truth.

Subject: Rudy
Sentence tells about: what Rudy knows

Circle the subject of each sentence.

1. The camp is located on Lake Walla Walla Bing Bang.

2. Woovis is head counselor at the camp.

3. The campers stay for two weeks at a time.

4. The rabbit bunkhouse is located deep underground.

5. The front of the bunkhouse has a picture of a rabbit on it.

6. On the other hand, the squirrel bunkhouse is in a tree.

7. Frog campers stay on lily pads near the lake.

8. Different campers eat different kinds of food.

9. The rabbits munch on lettuce.

10. Nuts are the favorite snack for the squirrels.

11. Unlike the others, the frogs catch their own food—flies.

12. Doesn't Camp Walla Walla Bing Bang sound like fun?

Name: _____

DOWN ON THE FARM featuring Woovis and Squirmy

YOU ANSWER IT!

Some sentences are more ridiculous than others. But all sentences have a subject and a verb. Can you find the subjects and verbs in the sentences above?

GRAMMAR WORKSHOP

What are the subject and verb? The subject identifies what the sentence is about. The verb tells you what happens in a sentence.

Sentence: The old tractor broke down last week.
Simple Subject: tractor
Verb: broke

Underline each subject. Circle each verb.

1. The trouble began last week.

2. The old tractor made all sorts of funny noises.

3. The noises continued all day.

4. Finally, the thing just stopped.

5. On the way to the tractor store, Woovis spotted a cow.

6. Woovis wondered what it would be like to have a cow.

7. Now Woovis was torn in two directions.

8. The farm needed a tractor.

9. What should he do?

10. In the end, Woovis bought a tractor.

DIGGER featuring Woovis and Ant Betty

YOU ANSWER IT!

Not all fragments are the same. Some fragments are *sentence fragments.* Can you find a sentence fragment in this cartoon?

GRAMMAR WORKSHOP

What is a sentence fragment? A sentence fragment is not a complete sentence. It does not have both a subject and a verb.

Fragment: A very smart ant
Sentence: Betty is a very smart ant.
Fragment: Dug up a metal object.
Sentence: Woovis dug up a metal object.

Write SENTENCE or FRAGMENT in the space provided for each group of words.

1. The most valuable ancient treasure of all. _____

2. Night and day the dog worked and worked. _____

3. Underneath ten feet of dirt, covered with rubble. _____

4. Could this be what we were looking for? _____

5. Digging through the sand, searching for gold. _____

6. A top scientist in his field. _____

7. Underground rocks jammed the power drill. _____

8. The unchanging underground temperature of 54 degrees. _____

9. Are you ready? _____

Name: _____

A PAINT STORY featuring Woovis and Rowena

YOU ANSWER IT!

Rowena's joke contains a run-on sentence. Can you correct it?

GRAMMAR WORKSHOP

What is a run-on sentence? A **run-on sentence** is a sentence with two complete thoughts that run together. Correct a run-on sentence by breaking it up into separate sentences.

Run-on: Rowena and Woovis are friends they jog together twice a week.

Rewrite each run-on sentence correctly.

1. Woovis loved jogging it was only natural that a dog loved to run.

_____

2. Jogging was more difficult for Rowena, pigs were not natural runners.

_____

3. Running was Woovis's favorite sport he also liked racquetball.

_____

4. Rowena did not like racquetball she didn't understand it, either.

_____

Name: _____

ROWENA THE EDITOR featuring Woovis and Rowena

YOU ANSWER IT!

Rowena overlooks more than just her nose. She also overlooks some fragments and run-on sentences in this cartoon. Can you find them?

GRAMMAR WORKSHOP

What is a fragment? A sentence fragment is an incomplete sentence. It does not have both a subject and a verb.

<u>Fragment</u>: A top-notch editor
<u>Sentence</u>: Rowena is a top-notch editor.

What is a run-on sentence? A run-on sentence has two complete thoughts that run together without conjunctions or correct punctuation.
Run-on: I'm tired, I want to go home.
Not a run-on: I'm tired. I want to go home.
        or
I'm tired and I want to go home.

Identify each sentence as a fragment (f) or a run-on (r-o) in the spaces provided on the right. Then rewrite each sentence in the spaces below.

1. Rowena's ad in the newspaper for an editor. ____

_____

2. Rowena is a great editor, she can edit anything. ____

_____

3. Rowena, who is known far and wide for her editing. ____

_____

4. Rowena is known as the best, who could be better? ____

_____

5. Woovis bringing in a real mess of a report. ____

_____

6. No one could fix Woovis's report then Rowena gave it a try. ____

_____

Name: _____

PHONE CALL featuring Molly and Squirmy

YOU ANSWER IT!

In this phone call, subjects and verbs don't always agree. Can you find the sentence in which the verb doesn't fit the subject?

GRAMMAR WORKSHOP

How do subjects and verbs agree?

Singular subjects take singular verbs.
<u>Wrong</u>: One parent **are** at home.   <u>Right</u>: One parent **is** at home.

Plural subjects take plural verbs.
<u>Wrong</u>: Both parents **is** at home.   <u>Right</u>: Both parents **are** at home.
<u>Wrong</u>: Molly and Squirmy **plays** games.   <u>Right</u>: Molly and Squirmy **play** games.

Circle the correct form of the verb.

1. Molly and Squirmy (is/are) good friends.

2. For a mouse, Molly (talk/talks) on the phone quite a bit.

3. Squirmy (don't/doesn't) talk very much on the phone.

4. Molly and her family (has/have) two telephone lines.

5. Sometimes, Squirmy (get/gets) a busy signal on both lines.

6. Woovis and Moovis (call/calls) Squirmy on the phone.

7. No one (is/are) home.

8. The answering machine (pick/picks) up the call.

28

Name: _____

BANK ROBBERY featuring Squirmy and Woovis

YOU ANSWER IT!

Squirmy's ideas about robbers may be a bit strange, but at least he doesn't have problems with subject and verb agreement. Can you find the mistake that Woovis made?

GRAMMAR WORKSHOP

· ·

How do subjects and verbs agree when the subject is hard to find?
In "here", "there", and "where" sentences, the subject (socks) can come after the verb.

Wrong: Here <u>is</u> my socks. (subject: socks)
Right: Here <u>are</u> my socks. (subject: socks)
In other sentences, a singular subject can have more than one part. Likewise, a plural subject can have one part.
   One of my toes <u>is</u> bent. (subject: one)
   Many fingers on my hand <u>are</u> crooked. (subject: fingers)

Circle the correct form of the verb in each sentence.

1. A group of robbers (enter/enters) the Worm National Bank.

2. Where (is/are) all the bank guards?

3. One of the three robbers (look/looks) familiar.

4. "Where (is/are) the bank vaults?" they demand.

5. Three guards and the bank president (take/takes) them to the vaults.

6. Two of the robbers (work/works) on cracking the combination to the safe.

7. The three-number combination (is/are) 15-34-28.

8. The leader of the robbers (break/breaks) into the vault.

9. There (is/are) an unexpected ending to the story.

10. These thieves (is/are) not lawbreakers.

Name: _____

THE FOREVER GARDEN featuring Harry and Squirmy

YOU ANSWER IT!

One sentence in this cartoon has both a direct object and an indirect object. Can you find them?

GRAMMAR WORKSHOP

What is a direct object? A direct object receives a verb's action or the result of that action.

Direct object: Harry planted a <u>flower</u>.
Direct object: Squirmy wore a big <u>hat</u>.

What is an indirect object? An indirect object comes before a direct object and identifies the receiver of the verb's action.

Indirect object: Harry gave <u>Squirmy</u> a lovely bouquet of artificial roses.

Circle the direct object in each sentence.

1. Harry bought a package of artificial tulips.

2. Harry dug a hole in the ground.

3. Squirmy and Harry planted the flowers in the ground.

4. Everyone enjoyed the flowers.

5. Harry poured water on the flowers even though they were fake.

Circle each direct object. Underline each indirect object.

6. Squirmy gave Harry some fake roses.

7. Harry showed Woovis the roses.

8. Harry gave the roses sunshine but no water.

9. Harry showed his friends the best way to keep fake roses healthy.

10. Harry now tells everyone his story about the roses.

Review Section 2

Identify each sentence as declarative, interrogative, imperative, or exclamatory. Then circle the subject and underline the verb in each sentence.

1. After graduating from the Dog Academy, Woovis decided to start his own rock and roll band.

2. Did you know how hard it is to make it in the music business?

3. Follow your heart wherever it takes you.

4. Woovis finally arrived in New York City!

5. Was that a good time for rock and roll bands?

6. Woovis met Molly Mouse, the agent.

Identify each exercise as a complete sentence, fragment, or run-on. Then rewrite the sentence, if necessary. Circle the direct object of each complete sentence.

7. Molly, a very popular figure in the music business.

8. Molly saw immediately that Woovis had little talent, she didn't tell him that, though.

9. Working hard, day and night, never stopping.

10. Woovis played his guitar all the time.

11. Finally, they got their big break, they played a gig at the Mouse Club.

Circle the correct form of the verb.

12. Woovis and his band (play/plays) very badly.

13. Most of the scouts in the audience (fall/falls) asleep.

14. "Your band (has/have) no talent," Molly tells Woovis.

15. "Maybe you and all the scouts (is/are) right," Woovis says.

Part 3:

USING PUNCTUATION

LIVE AT HA-HA'S featuring Woovis

Woovis Live! at Ha Ha Comedy Club

A farmer hires a bunch of elephants to walk all over his potato field.

Finally, one of the elephants asks the farmer, "Why do you want us to trample your potato crop?

The farmer says, I'm trying to grow MASHED potatoes." Get it?

Har har.

Yuk yuk!

Ha ha.

YOU ANSWER IT!

Woovis tells a good joke, but he missed some quotation marks. Can you find them?

(see page 41)

Name: _____

DAKOTA featuring Monica and Rudy

YOU ANSWER IT!

Monica has trouble with capitals. Can you find her mistakes?

GRAMMAR WORKSHOP

When do you use capitals?

Use capitals to begin a sentence.
- Every state has a capital.

Use capitals for proper nouns that name a particular person, place, or thing.
- Pierre is the capital of South Dakota.
- Jane Chung is the mayor of Pierre.
- I've known Mayor Chung for two years.

Rewrite each sentence using capitals correctly.

1. "i just love Parties," monica said.

_____

2. rudy's favorite party Game is pin-the-tail-on-the-Donkey.

_____

3. last Year's game in charlotte, North carolina, didn't go so well.

_____

4. rudy accidentally pinned the tail on a real donkey named dr. Winston.

_____

Name: _____

HAT REPLACEMENT featuring Judy and Woovis

YOU ANSWER IT!

Woovis made a mistake with Judy's hat, and with commas! Can you find his mistakes?

GRAMMAR WORKSHOP

How do you use commas in a series of items? Use commas after each item to separate three or more items.

Correct: Judy's hat was torn, tattered, battered, and bashed.
Don't use commas to separate only two items.
Correct: Woovis's offer was kind and generous.

Add commas to punctuate each sentence correctly. Cross out unneeded commas.

1. Judy lent Woovis a hat boots and, suspenders for the big dance.

2. Frogs, dogs and cats were all invited, to the dance.

3. Woovis danced with two frogs, and three cats.

4. Everyone peacefully danced pranced and visited, for a while.

5. The trouble began when one cat hissed, and growled, at a dog.

6. The dog chased the cat out the door past the parking lot, and into the barn.

7. Everyone followed behind, hopping running and chasing after the two.

8. Woovis' hat fell off as he watched the dog, chase the cat, over the bridge under the hedge and through the garden.

Name: _____

SKATING ALONG featuring Woovis and Rowena

I took my first ice-skating lesson in Chicago Illinois on December 12 1999.

Oh yeah. What do you find to be the hardest thing about learning to skate?

The ice!

YOU ANSWER IT!

Rowena needs to learn a thing or two about skating. She also needs to learn about commas. Can you find the comma errors she made?

GRAMMAR WORKSHOP

How do you use commas in dates and places? Set off the year with commas. At the end of a sentence you need only one comma. In the middle of a sentence you need to use two commas.

Right: I was born on May 1, 1994.
Right: On May 1, 1994, I was born.

Use the same pattern with places. Set off the state or country with commas.

Right: I was born in Milan, Ohio.
Right: Milan, Ohio, is where I was born.

Write missing commas in the correct places.

1. Before March 15 1989 no pig had ever ice skated.

2. Rowena's great-grandfather invented skates for pigs on March 15 1989.

3. He tested the pig skates on a lake in Bryan Ohio.

4. Pigs from as far away as Detroit Michigan came to watch.

5. Word of the successful test spread as far as London England.

Cross out the unnecessary commas. Write missing commas in the correct places.

6. On January, 15, 1999 pigs celebrated the first Skate Day.

7. The celebration started in Las, Vegas Nevada.

8. From there, it spread to Berkeley California and Boise Idaho.

9. In Tokyo, Japan pigs held a 24-hour Skate-a-thon.

10. On January 15, 2009 pigs will celebrate the 10th annual Skate Day.

TRUE TALE featuring Rowena and Friends

ROWENA'S TRUE STORY HOUR

And then there was the time when I was trapped in a cave with only three things: a calendar a bed and a clock.

Wow! How did you survive?

Well for food I ate dates off the calendar. When I was thirsty I drank water from the bed springs....

And finally, when I wanted more I just got "seconds" from the clock.

Wow.

YOU ANSWER IT!

Rowena's story is not only silly. It also misuses commas! How many comma mistakes can you find?

GRAMMAR WORKSHOP

. . . .

When do you use commas?

1. To seperate a list of three or more items:
• Squirmy, Molly, and Ant Betty came to listen.
2. To separate two or more adjectives:
• Tall, rangy pigs are hard to find.
3. To join clauses after the words for, but, and, or, nor, and yet:
• I'm hungry, but I won't eat dates.
4. To set off phrases that begin or interrupt a sentence:
• After dinner, they all had seconds.
• Rowena, a pig, tells wonderful stories.

Write in the missing commas for each sentence.

1. Rowena's story hour is short fun and entertaining.

2. Most of Rowena's stories are about young smart pigs.

3. Rowena was once a young pig herself but now she is almost grown up.

4. Each night Rowena tells a different story.

5. Squirmy a young worm, loves to listen to stories.

Cross out the unnecessary commas. Write missing commas in the correct places.

6. How can one pig all by herself tell all those, stories?

7. On Halloween Rowena, tells spooky stories.

8. One especially spooky story, *Ghost Pig* is about a spooky pig.

37

Name: _____

GRAMMAR AND GRAMPS featuring Judy and Molly

YOU ANSWER IT!

Both Molly and Judy made mistakes with contractions. Can you find them? Circle each error.

GRAMMAR WORKSHOP

What is a contraction? A **contraction** combines two words with an apostrophe. The apostrophe is used to replace missing letters.

Examples:

Haven't you heard... (Have not)
I'm going to visit... (I am)
They're in Florida... (They are)
I'll be seeing... (I will)
You still **don't**... (do not)

In each sentence, underline the contraction that is spelled correctly.

1. Molly (hasnt/hasn't) seen her grandparents since they moved away.

2. Up north, her grandparents' mouse hole (wasn't/was'nt) very fancy.

3. Once they got to Florida, it (didn't/did'nt) take them long to find a condo.

4. The condo (they're/theyr'e) living in now has a picture window, air-conditioning, and a cheese cellar full of rare cheeses.

5. "We (haven't/have'nt) been this happy in ages," says Gramma.

THE LOST BALLOON featuring Judy, Monica, and Harry

YOU ANSWER IT!

Location is a problem for Judy and Monica in more ways than one. Can you find the location of the missing apostrophe?

GRAMMAR WORKSHOP

What is a possessive? A possessive is a word that shows ownership. Most possessives use an apostrophe.

Singular: one bear's friend, one frog's balloon, one bus's tire
Plural: two bears' friend, two frogs' balloon, two buses' tires, the children's money

Fill in the missing apostrophes in the following sentences.

1. It was Judys idea to get a balloon and sail around the world.

2. She read about ballooning in Woovis magazine.

3. The balloon kits price was $150.

4. Money from Monicas piggy bank paid for the balloon kit.

5. The two friends job was to build the balloon.

6. In two weeks time, they had the balloon ready to go.

7. The purple and red balloon captured peoples attention everywhere.

8. The launch was spurred on by the audiences cheers.

9. The two explorers plan was immediately upset by a leaky balloon.

10. Shortly after they took off, the balloons leak blew them off course.

11. The two adventurers response to all this trouble was to keep calm.

Name: _____

STREET SMARTS featuring Squirmy and Ant Betty

YOU ANSWER IT!

Squirmy makes a mistake using a possessive pronoun in the first panel. Can you find it?

GRAMMAR WORKSHOP

What is a possessive? *Possessives are words that show ownership. Possessive nouns take an apostrophe. Possessive pronouns do not use an apostrophe.*

Singular nouns: cat's paw, child's foot
Plural nouns: cats' paws, children's feet
Possessive pronouns: my foot: mine, your hat: yours, her pen: hers, its size: its, our pet: ours, your shirts: yours, their cups: theirs

Circle the correct possessive form in each sentence.

1. Ant Betty loves (Squirmys, Squirmy's) jokes.

2. She often repeats the jokes as if they were (her's/hers).

3. "When I tell a joke many times I feel that it's (mine/mines)," she says.

4. "The jokes are part (your's/yours) and part mine," Squirmy says.

5. Some of the ant (colony's/colonies) favorite jokes are about people.

6. "Ants love to laugh at (people's/peoples') flaws," Ant Betty says.

7. "We ants feel that your flaws are similar to (our's/ours)," she adds.

Name: _____

LIVE AT HA-HA'S featuring Woovis

GRAMMAR WORKSHOP

When do you use quotation marks? Use two quotation marks at the beginning and end of the speaker's words. Start each quotation with a capital letter.

Wrong: Woovis said, "let's eat.
Right: Woovis said, "Let's eat."
Wrong: That's funny!" Molly cried.
Right: "That's funny!" Molly cried.

Insert quotation marks in the correct place in each sentence. Correct capitalization mistakes.

1. Welcome to the Ha-Ha Comedy Club, Woovis said.

2. Tonight I'll be telling you some of my finest jokes, added Woovis.

3. A skunk in the audience asked, Can you tell some jokes about skunks?

4. Woovis said, Hmm. I know one skunk joke, but it's a real stinker.

5. Tell it anyway, said the skunk. I love skunk jokes.

6. The mouse said, excuse me but I'd like to hear some mouse jokes.

7. Mouse jokes aren't funny, said the alligator. I'd rather hear gator jokes.

8. Alligator jokes stink! cried the skunk. can't you tell more skunk jokes?

Name: _____

WOODEN SHOE featuring Woovis

YOU ANSWER IT!

Woovis included some quotation marks in his joke, but he made a punctuation mistake. Can you find it?

GRAMMAR WORKSHOP

How do you punctuate quotations? Here are some examples.
Begin quotations with a capital letter unless they continue a sentence.

Wrong: "Yes," said Bo, "That is correct."
Right: "Yes," said Bo, "that is correct."
Put end marks *inside* of quotation marks.
Wrong: "I'm back"! Wally said.
Right: "I'm back!" Wally said.
Introduce quotations with a comma.
Wrong: Maddy asked "Who's home?"
Right: Maddy asked, "Who's home?"

In the following sentences, insert missing quotation marks and other punctuation. Correct capitalization mistakes.

1. Squirmy asked Woovis, can we interview you for *Weekly Blab* magazine?

2. sure, Woovis said, that sounds like a great idea.

3. How does it feel to be a famous comedian Squirmy inquired.

4. I'm not all that famous, Woovis said. I've never been on TV.

5. Molly added I've heard that the networks want to give you your own show.

6. It's possible Woovis replied. I'm not sure I'm ready for my own show.

Name: _____

OH IOWA featuring Judy and Squirmy

GRAMMAR WORKSHOP

One use for apostrophes is to show the difference between words that sound alike with the same or similar spellings, but with different meanings (homonyms).

Sound-alike
it's (it is, it has)
you're (you are)
they're (they are)

there's (there is)
let's (let us)
we're (we are)

Sound-alike
its (belongs to it)
your (belongs to you)
their (belongs to them)
there (in that place)
theirs (belongs to them)
lets (allows)
were (existed in past)

Circle the correct form of each word.

1. Animal Jeopardy has (its/it's) own set of special rules.

2. (Your/You're) answer must be stated in the form of a question.

3. All players must give (their/there) answers as questions.

4. Each question should have (it's/its) own question mark.

5. (Its/It's) easy to forget and give an answer rather than a question.

Name: _____

Review Section 3

Correct mistakes in using capitals, commas, apostrophes, and quotation marks.
Cross out mistakes. Write in all missing punctuation.

1. woovis' his rock and roll band was not good at singing playing or Dancing.

2. On march 30 2000 Woovis dissolved the band.

3. At that point Woovis had no job no money and no car.

4. so Woovis went to hollywood california to see his friend Rowena.

5. Rowenas job was to Read movie script's.

6. "Were looking for good scripts about dogs, rowena said.

7. "hey, Im a dog! Woovis cried.

8. Woovis said Youre looking at your next big screenwriter."

9. for three, months Woovis worked feverishly on his script.

10. "Its the story of a dog who is handsome smart and talented Woovis said.

11. "by any chance could that Dog be You? rowena asked.

12. Dont be ridiculous!" Woovis said.

13. By august 5 2000 the dogs script was finished.

14. Rowena gave it to a big movie Director named Lefty Lewis.

15. "in my opinion its really a lousy script" Lefty said.

16. Rowena tried other readers but they felt the same way.

17. you're script is no good," Rowena told Woovis.

18. "oh well back to the drawing board" Woovis said.

Part 4:
USING VERBS

MODERN ART featuring Woovis and Betty

YOU ANSWER IT!

Some paintings are more regular than others. So are some verbs. Find the mistake that Ant Betty made using an irregular verb.

(see page 47)

Name: _____

WOOVIS' POETRY CORNER featuring Woovis

Okay, class! Let's read today's poem.

Today's Poem

I see a cloud
And as I go
I catch my foot
And stub my toe

The poem describes a CLOUD and a STUBBED TOE. How do the two compare?

The cloud pours with rain...

While the stubbed toe roars with pain!

Haw!

YOU ANSWER IT!

While Woovis compares a cloud and a toe, you can compare verb tenses. What verb tense is used in Today's Poem?

GRAMMAR WORKSHOP

What are some verb tenses? The present, past, present progressive, and present perfect are important verb tenses. Each tense is shown below.

Present: run, runs
Past: ran
Present perfect: have/has run,
Present progressive: am/is/are running
Future: will run

Identify each underlined verb as present, past, present perfect, or present progressive.

1. Woovis <u>wrote</u> Today's Poem himself. _____

2. Woovis <u>has</u> <u>written</u> dozens of poems. _____

3. Some of the poems <u>rhyme</u>. _____

4. Other poems <u>make</u> no sense at all. _____

5. Once, Woovis wrote a poem that <u>sounded</u> like a honking goose. _____

6. Woovis <u>is</u> <u>gaining</u> fame as a poet all over the world. _____

7. In Japan, they <u>call</u> him "The Rhyme Dog." _____

8. In France, they soon <u>will</u> <u>award</u> Woovis a medal of honor. _____

46

Name: _____

MODERN ART featuring Woovis and Betty

YOU ANSWER IT!

Some paintings are more regular than others. So are some verbs. Find the mistake that Ant Betty made using an irregular verb.

GRAMMAR WORKSHOP : *What are regular and irregular verbs?* Regular verbs have past tense forms that end in -ed or -d. Irregular verbs have unusual past tense forms.

	verb	past	past participle
Regular:	work	worked	have worked
Regular:	hope	hoped	have hoped
Irregular:	sell	sold	have sold
Irregular:	go	went	have gone
Irregular:	know	knew	have known
Irregular:	get	got	have gotten

Circle the correct form of each verb in parentheses.

1. Woovis (painted/paint) for many years as an unknown.

2. Finally, after all that work, he (selled/sold) his first painting.

3. Woovis had (hope/hoped) to get a hundred dollars for the work.

4. If Woovis had (got/gotten) even five dollars for the painting, he would have been happy.

5. Three years ago, Woovis (go/went) to Paris to study art.

6. There, he (speak/spoke) to some of the world's great artists.

7. They all (tell/told) him that he had absolutely no talent.

Name: _____

SUPERSTITION featuring Monica and Rudy

Are you superstitious?

Nope. I never have been superstitious. I never will be superstitious.

How come?

Because it's bad luck.

YOU ANSWER IT!

Rudy's ideas about superstition may not make perfect sense, but Rudy does use the perfect tense. Can you find where he uses it?

GRAMMAR WORKSHOP

. . . .

What is the perfect tense? The perfect tense has three forms: present perfect, past perfect, and future perfect.

Present perfect: has/have spoken
Past perfect: had spoken
Future perfect: will have spoken

Circle the correct form of the perfect tense in each sentence.

1. Monica always (has/had) felt that superstition is an important topic.

2. In the past, Rudy never (had/has) worried about superstition.

3. Now, Rudy (has/will have) started to worry that he could be superstitious.

4. Last year, Rudy (hasn't/hadn't) worried about seeing a black cat.

5. By this time next year, Rudy (have/will have) thought through these matters more carefully.

Cross out the verb used incorrectly in each sentence. Write the correct verb above the cross-out.

6. Until I was ten, I never have stepped on a sidewalk crack.

7. I never had walked under a ladder.

8. Whenever Rudy has worried about things going wrong, he had knocked on wood.

LIARS AND LAYERS featuring Moovis and Squirmy

YOU ANSWER IT!

Moovis may think she never lies, but she is lying right now. Can you explain why these characters are confused?

GRAMMAR WORKSHOP

When do you use lie and lay? Lie means to rest by stretching out. Another meaning of lie is to say something that is false. Lay means to put something down.

Present	Past	Participles
lie (recline)	lay	lying, have lain
lay (put down)	laid	laying, have laid
lie (speak falsely)	lied	lying, have lied

Notice that lie never has a direct object while lay may have a direct object.
I lay on the floor. (no direct object)
I laid the hat down. (direct object: hat)

Circle the correct word in parentheses.

1. When she has important thinking to do, Moovis likes to (lie/lay) down on the barn floor.

2. Yesterday, Moovis (lie/lay) on the barn floor for a long time.

3. Wooden boards have been (lain/laid) over the barn floor to keep it clean.

4. Moovis decided that it would be a good idea to (lie/lay) a carpet over the boards.

5. (Lying/Laying) on carpet is more comfortable than (lying/laying) on a board floor.

6. "Have you ever (laid/lain) carpet before?" asked Squirmy.

Name: _____

COLD SPELL featuring Woovis and Rowena

YOU ANSWER IT!

Woovis may know a lot about boots, but he doesn't know much about the verbs *sit* and *set*. Can you find the mistake in the cartoon above?

GRAMMAR WORKSHOP

When *do* you use *sit* and *set*? Sit means to rest in an upright position. Set means to put or place something.

Present	Past	Participles
sit (rest)	sat	sitting, have sat
set (put)	set	setting, have set

When *do* you use *rise* and *raise*? Rise means to go up. Raise means to lift up or cause to rise.

Present	Past	Participle
rise (go up)	rose	rising, have risen
raise (lift up)	raised	raising, have raised

Circle the correct form of **sit** *or* **set**, **rise** *or* **raise** *in each sentence.*

1. Rowena (set/sat) down at the boot store.

2. She watched the clerk (set/sit) items in the display case.

3. Rowena (rose/raised) her hand.

4. "I have been (sitting/setting) here for 20 minutes," she said.

5. The clerk (raised/rose) from his seat.

6. Then the clerk (sat/set) a single red rose next to Rowena's chair.

50

Review Section 4

Identify the tense of each underlined verb as present, past, perfect, or progressive.
Label each perfect tense verb as present, past, or future.

1. After failing in Hollywood, Woovis <u>goes</u> to New York. _____

2. "I'm <u>feeling</u> pretty down on myself then," Woovis says. _____

3. Then Woovis <u>met</u> an editor named Ginny. _____

4. "I'm <u>looking</u> for a dog to be in a book," Ginny says. _____

5. Woovis never <u>had appeared</u> in a book before. _____

6. "<u>I will have organized</u> my own rock band by next year,"

   he tells Ginny. _____

Choose the correct form of each verb.

7. At first, Woovis just needs to (sit/set) there and observe everyone.

8. "I (raised/rose) every morning at seven and barely said a word by noon," Woovis
   said.

9. "For the first time, I (told/telled) jokes on stage," Woovis said.

10. "I had never (went/gone) before a live audience before," Woovis said..

11. "It had (got/gotten) to the point where I was so nervous I couldn't speak," Woovis
    said.

12. "That's not true," Ginny said. "Woovis was a complete natural on stage. He
    (speaked/spoke) well and handled himself perfectly."

Part 5:
SPECIAL TOPICS

THE MATTERPAL featuring Monica and Rudy

YOU ANSWER IT!

This cartoon has some mistakes that the proofreader must have missed. Can you find them?

(see page 58)

Name: _____

THE SEA BISCUIT featuring Woovis and Rudy

Can you find two comparative forms of the word *good* in this cartoon?

GRAMMAR WORKSHOP

What are comparatives and superlatives? A comparative compares one item or group to another. A superlative compares three or more items.

Word	comparative	superlative
loud	louder	loudest
tough	tougher	toughest
terrible	more terrible	most terrible
good	better	best
bad	worse	worst

Circle the correct form of each comparative word in parentheses.

1. The Sea Biscuit is the (good/better/best) boat Woovis has ever had.

2. It has a (nice/nicer/nicest) design than Woovis's old boat, the Leaky Wreck.

3. The Leaky Wreck had a (terrible/more terrible/most terrible) leaking problem.

4. This Leaky Wreck had (many/more/most) holes than a piece of Swiss cheese.

5. Water leaked into the Leaky Wreck (fast/faster/fastest) than it leaked out.

6. Sea Biscuit is (faster/fastest/more faster) than the Leaky Wreck.

7. The Leaky Wreck is the (ugly/uglier/ugliest) boat in town.

Name: _____

STUDENT DRIVER featuring Rowena and Squirmy

YOU ANSWER IT!

Rowena has a lot to learn about driving. She also needs to learn about double negatives. Can you find the double negative in this cartoon?

GRAMMAR WORKSHOP

. . . .

How do you correct double negatives? Replace two negatives with a single negative.
Wrong: I don't have no money.
Right: I don't have any money.
Wrong: He couldn't hardly run.
Right: He could hardly run.
How do you correct double comparisons? Replace two modifiers with a single modifier.
Wrong: Squirmy is a more better driver.
Right: Squirmy is a better driver.

Circle the correct words in parentheses for each sentence.

1. Rowena is not the (most skillful/most skillfullest) bike rider around.

2. She hasn't got (any/no) sense of the road.

3. In some ways, riding a bike is (more harder/harder) than driving a car.

4. For one thing, you don't have (no/any) turn signals.

5. The (most easiest/easiest) thing to do is use hand signals for turns.

6. Rowena can't (never/ever) figure out which hand signal to use.

7. Fortunately, she never rides (more faster/faster) than two miles per hour.

8. At this speed, even if she hits something, she (could/couldn't) hardly cause a danger to anyone.

Name: _____

HOMEMADE DONUTS featuring Molly and Ant Betty

This donut is good. Who made it?

I did.

You cook good. Did you make the whole thing?

Except for the hole in the middle...

That was already there!

YOU ANSWER IT!

Molly is good at eating donuts, but she is not so good at using the words *good* and *well*. Can you find the mistake she made?

GRAMMAR WORKSHOP

When do you use good and well? *Use good as an adjective to modify nouns or pronouns. Use well to modify verbs. Well can also modify a noun when it refers to someone's health.*

1. **Wrong:** Ant Betty cooks <u>good</u>.
2. **Right:** Ant Betty cooks <u>well</u>.
3. **Wrong:** The donuts are <u>well</u>.
4. **Right:** The donuts are <u>good</u>.
5. **Right:** Ant Betty feels <u>well</u> today.

Complete each sentence by writing good or well in the space provided.

1. Ant Betty found a _____ recipe in the Insect Cookbook.

2. Ant Betty works _____ with recipes that include a lot of sugar.

3. Ant Betty follows recipe directions _____.

4. The donuts turned out _____ after cooking for 35 minutes.

5. Ant Betty left the donut out for two days and it was still _____.

6. Ant Betty cooks only when she is healthy and feels _____.

7. A donut goes _____ with a glass of cold milk.

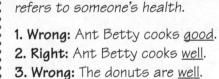

Name: _____

THE MIGHTY ANT featuring Ant Betty and Squirmy

I'm one of the world's strongest ants. I can hold up the wait of this giant sugar cube for one hour!

Wow!

I know something that ways less than that cube—but I bet you can't hold it for five minutes!

What's that?

Your breath!

YOU ANSWER IT!

No matter how strong you are, you can get mixed up with words that sound alike. Can you find the homophone mistakes in this cartoon?

GRAMMAR WORKSHOP

. . . .

Homophones are words that sound alike, but have different spellings and meanings.

wait (delay) and
weight (heaviness)
accept (to receive) and
except (all but)
affect (to influence) and
effect (result)
here (in this place) and
hear (listen)
lead (metal) and
led (what leader did)
passed (went by) and
past (earlier time)
piece (part of) and
peace (no war)

In each sentence, circle the correct word in the parentheses.

1. Ant Betty is strong in many (ways/weighs).

2. She practices her weightlifting every day (accept/except) Monday.

3. Ant Betty (lead/led) a campaign called Power Ants to help ants get in shape.

4. She has put on shows in the (passed/past) to raise money for Power Ants.

5. In one show, Ant Betty lifted a one-ounce (piece/peace) of wood.

6. Ant Betty's (affect/effect) on audiences is amazing.

7. People cheer so loud for her that you can't (here/hear) yourself think.

8. Next month, Ant Betty will try to lift a three-ounce (led/lead) pipe!

Name: _____

THE MATTERPAL featuring Monica and Rudy

YOU ANSWER IT!

This cartoon has some mistakes that the proofreader must have missed. Can you find them?

GRAMMAR WORKSHOP : *What do you look to correct when you proofread?* Things to look for include:

Capitalization: monica → Monica
Punctuation: commas, question marks, periods, apostrophes, and others
Other mistakes:
  • Run-on sentences, fragments
Grammar mistakes:
  • I ain't going. → I'm not going.

Proofread each sentence. Look for punctuation and capitalization errors. Mark each correction. Add or cross out words to make corrections when necessary.

1. The Title of monicas storybook is bearly Tales.

2. The Book is about a Bear named Monica?

3. in the book, monica roams through the forest searching for Honey.

4. she climbs up an Oak Tree and gets stuck between two branches,

5. "Help." monica shouts!" but no one can hear her?

6. Monica gets stuck in the tree since she is stuck she decides to eat the honey.

7. Stuck in the tree for several hours without anyone in sight.

JOB INTERVIEW featuring Judy and Rowena

I need a job.

let me ask you some editing questions. What sentence has 100 letters?

This sentence: the mail carrier has 100 letters in her mail bag.

Okay. What sentence has no letters?

the mail carrier dropped her mail bag in the river

Rowena's Editing Service

You're hired.

Good, because I just got fired from the post office!

YOU ANSWER IT!

Judy may answer the all questions correctly, but she does make some editing errors. Find the proofreading mistakes in this cartoon.

GRAMMAR WORKSHOP

What do you look to correct when you proofread? Things to look for include:

Capitalization: rowena ⟶ Rowena
Punctuation: commas, question marks, periods, apostrophes, and others
Other things to correct:
- run-on sentences, fragments
- missing words
- grammar mistakes
- spelling mistakes
- sentences that don't make sense
- paragraph and indentation mistakes

Proofread the story below. Correct mistakes by crossing out words and adding new words.

My New Job by Judy the Frog, Editor

I was hired by Rowena on May 5 1999. what a day that was! rowena put me to work right away my first job ws to edit a book about Pigs called the Wonderful, wonderful pig. Ill tell ya, I was really scared at first. Because I knew NOTHING about pigs! Howevre, I learned alot from editing the book. For exampel, did you know that Pigs are one of the most intellijent animals. They really are. It took three week's to edit the book. I Learned a lot about Pigs. I also Learned many important editing skills. I will use these skills to edit my next book. It's title is the Wonderful, Wonderful frog.

Review Section 5

Circle the correct words in parentheses for each sentence.

1. Woovis's first book was the (good/better/best) he ever did.

2. "It was a math book," Woovis said, "and I didn't have (no/any) experience with math."

3. Things turned out (good/well) only because Woovis worked every day for 14 hours or more.

4. "When the book was finished I was ready to (except/accept) total failure," Woovis said.

5. Everyone thought a math book with cartoon characters was the (strangest/most strangest) thing they'd ever heard of.

6. The reviews for the book came out and almost none of them were (good/well).

7. But people bought the book and one sale (lead/led) to another.

Proofread each sentence. Mark and correct capitalization and punctuation mistakes. Fix run-ons and fragments.

8. suddenly we realized that the Book was, a hit?

9. Woovis became a star, he was mobbed wherever he went.

10. After dozens of Woovis books, movies, and TV appearances, the world's number-one celebrity dog.

ANSWERS

Heart-Shaped Pool (page 10)
You Answer It!: 2 nouns—swimming pool, water
1. Rowena | party | grand opening | swimming pool
2. party | Ant Betty | Insect World | swimming suit
3. Ant Betty | model | polka dots
4. beetle | Mavis | party | suit | Ant Betty
5. shock | embarrassment | Ant Betty
6. Ant Betty | chair | tea | lemon
7. thing | day | Rowena

Fix Your Wagon (page 11)
You Answer It!: were taking; flipped; come; will get; can fix; don't think; would like; is
1. Molly and Ant Betty <u>planned</u> a ride to town. (mental action)
2. The road <u>curved</u> sharply just outside of town. (action verb)
3. Molly and Ant Betty <u>spilled</u> over. (action verb)
4. "Yow!" Ant Betty <u>cried</u>. (action verb)
5. No one <u>was</u> hurt (verb of being)
(6–8: Answers will vary)
6. *rode*   7. *purchased*
8. *went*

Not Your Cheese (page 12)
You Answer It!: You; I; What; you; you; I; What; it; I; it
1. them   2. they
3. Nobody   4. This
5. I   6. you
7. They   8. this
9. Everyone

Sick Tree (page 13)
You Answer It!: you and her
(Parentheses indicate deletions)
1. us
2. He
3. They
4. She and I
5. me
6. (me) I
7. (I) me
8. (me) I
9. (Us) We

Geography Time (page 14)
You Answer It!: Which one of the countries on the map *is* your favorite?
1. <u>Many</u>/are   2. <u>No one</u>/says
3. <u>Most</u>/are   4. <u>Nothing</u>/is
5. <u>One</u>/was   6. <u>Some</u>/study

Duck Soup (page 15)
You Answer It!: delicious
(Words in italics should be circled)
1. <u>dark</u>, <u>stormy</u>   2. <u>Strange</u>, <u>back</u>
3. <u>famous</u>, <u>green</u>   4. <u>horrid</u>   5. <u>disgusting</u>, <u>sickening</u>
6. *foul* (sink)
7. *quick, Soup* (Shop)
8. *full, bean* (soup)

Animal Jeopardy (page 16)
You Answer It!: mama, papa, brother, sister
(1-4 Answers will vary)

Moon Food! (page 17)
You Answer It!: recently
(Words in italics should be circled)
1. *quietly*   2. *casually*
3. *politely*   4. *thoroughly*
5. *very*   6. *slowly* (ate)
7. *gradually* (rose)   8. *frantically* (cried)
9. *terribly* (sorry)

The Beach (page 18)
You Answer It!: really, very
(1–10: Answers will vary)

Trash Time (page 19)
You Answer It: into
1. <u>at</u>   2. <u>with</u>
3. <u>for</u>   4. <u>inside</u>
5. <u>on</u>   6. <u>of</u>
7. <u>into</u> the swimming pool   8. <u>on</u> the watchband
9. <u>with</u> water.

Review Section 1 (page 20)
1. name | is | Woovis | dog
2. I | am | dog   (adj)
3. We | welcome | you | page   (adj)
4. We | wanted to make | page   (adj)
5. page | contains | problems | This   (adj)
6. It | contains | story | dog | Woovis (adv)
7. Woovis | came | city | farm | country (adj)
8. mother | said | Woovis | was | grammar (adv)
9. school | Woovis | was | student   (adj)
10. teachers | gave | Woovis | marks | grammar (adv)
11. Dogs | bark | they | speak   (adv)
12. Woovis | speaks | languages | English | dog-speak (adj)
13. were   14. are
15. was   16. have

(17-21: Answers will vary.)
17. *small*, in the country
18. *patiently*, for years
19. *popular*, in several magazines

Tree Knowledge (page 22)
You Answer It!: Bears know much more about trees than dogs. (declarative); I completely disagree! (exclamatory); Okay, then tell me what kind of tree this is. (imperative); How can you tell? (interrogative)
1. interrogative (?)   2. declarative (.)
3. imperative (.)   4. exclamatory (!)
5. declarative (.)   6. declarative (.)
7. imperative (.)   8. exclamatory (!)

Camp Walla Walla Bing Bang (page 23)
You Answer It!: The mosquitoes find you.

1.	camp	2.	Woovis
3.	campers	4.	bunkhouse
5.	bunkhouse	6.	bunkhouse
7.	campers	8.	campers
9.	rabbits	10.	Nuts
11.	frogs	12.	Camp Walla Walla Bing Bang

Down on the Farm (page 24)
You Answer It!: I/can decide; You/would look; it/would be; you/have
(Words in italics should be circled)

1.	<u>trouble</u> *began*	2.	<u>tractor</u> *made*
3.	<u>noises</u> *continued*	4.	<u>thing</u> *stopped*
5.	<u>Woovis</u> *spotted*	6.	<u>Woovis</u> *wondered*
7.	<u>Woovis</u> *was torn*	8	<u>farm</u> *needed*
9.	<u>he</u> *should do*	10.	<u>Woovis</u> *bought*

Digger (page 25)
You Answer It!: This fragment that says TWACK.

1.	fragment	2.	sentence
3.	fragment	4.	sentence
5.	fragment	6.	fragment
7.	sentence	8.	fragment
9.	sentence		

A Paint Story (page 26)
You Answer It!: Don't move. I've got you completely covered.
1. Woovis loved jogging. It was only natural that a dog loved to run.
2. Jogging was more difficult for Rowena. Pigs were not natural runners.
3. Running was Woovis' favorite sport. He also liked racquetball.
4. Rowena did not like racquetball. She didn't understand it, either.

Rowena the Editor (page 27)
You Answer It!: I'm totally careful. I never overlook a thing. I'll tell you something that you always overlook.
1. fragment (answers will vary)
2. run-on (Rowena is a great editor. She can edit anything.)
3. fragment (answers will vary)
4. run-on (Rowena is known as the best. Who could be better?)
5. fragment (answers will vary)
6. run-on (No one could fix Woovis's report. Then Rowena gave it a try.)

Phone Call (page 28)
You Answer It!: Is your parents at home? (are)

1.	are	2.	talks
3.	doesn't	4.	have
5.	gets	6.	call
7.	is	8.	picks

Bank Robbery! (page 29)
You Answer It!: There is bank robbers back there! (are)

1.	enters	2.	are
3.	looks	4.	are
5.	take	6.	work
7.	is	8.	breaks
9.	is	10.	are

The Forever Garden (page 30)
You Answer It!: I'm giving my flowers (indirect object) some water (direct object).

1.	package	2.	hole
3.	flowers	4.	flowers

5. water
(Words in italics should be circled)

6.	<u>Harry</u>, *roses*	7.	<u>Woovis</u>, *roses.*
8.	<u>roses</u>, *sunshine*	9.	<u>friends</u>, *way*
10.	<u>everyone</u>, *story*		

Review Section 2 (page 31)
(Words in italics should be circled)
1. *Woovis* <u>decided</u> (declarative)
2. *you* <u>did</u> <u>know</u> (interrogative)
3. *you* (implied) <u>Follow</u> (imperative)
4. *Woovis* <u>arrived</u> (exclamatory)
5. <u>Was</u> *that* (interrogative)
6. *Woovis* <u>met</u> (declarative)
7. Fragment (Answers will vary)
8. Run-on (Molly saw immediately that Woovis had little talent. She didn't tell him that, though.)
9. Fragment (Answers will vary)
10. Complete sentence, guitar (direct object)
11. Run-on (Finally, they got their big break. They played a gig at the Mouse Club.)

12.	play	13.	fall
14.	has	15.	are

Dakota (page 34)
You Answer It!: South Dakota should be capitalized.
1. "<u>I</u> just love <u>p</u>arties," Monica said.
2. <u>R</u>udy's favorite party game is <u>P</u>in-the-<u>T</u>ail-on-the-donkey.
3. <u>L</u>ast year's game in <u>C</u>harlotte, <u>N</u>orth <u>C</u>arolina, didn't go so well.
4. <u>R</u>udy accidentally pinned the tail on a real donkey named <u>D</u>r. Winston.

Hat Replacement (page 35)
You Answer It!: I accidentally bounced, smashed, and kicked it.
(Parentheses indicate deletions)
1. Judy lent Woovis a hat, boots, and(,) suspenders for the big dance.
2. Frogs, dogs, and cats were all invited(,) to the dance.
3. Woovis danced with two frogs(,) and three cats.
4. Everyone peacefully danced, pranced, and visited(,) for a while.
5. The trouble began when one cat hissed(,) and growled(,) at a dog.
6. The dog chased the cat out the door, past the parking lot, and into the barn.
7. Everyone followed behind, hopping, running, and chasing after the two.
8. Woovis' hat fell off as he watched the dog(,) chase the cat(,) over the bridge, under the hedge, and through the garden.

Skating Along (page 36)
You Answer It!: Chicago, Illinois, / December 12, 1999

1.	March 15, 1989,	2.	March 15, 1989
3.	Bryan, Ohio.	4.	Detroit, Michigan,
5.	London, England.		

(Parentheses indicate deletions)
6. On January(,) 15, 1999, pigs celebrated the first Skate Day.
7. The celebration started in Las(,) Vegas, Nevada.
8. From there, it spread to Berkeley, California, and

Boise, Idaho.

9. In Tokyo, Japan, pigs held a 24-hour Skate-a-thon.
10. On January 15, 2009, pigs will celebrate the 10th annual Skate Day.

True Tale (page 37)
You Answer It!: a calendar, a bed, and a clock; Well,; When I was thirsty,; when I wanted more,
1. Rowena's story hour is short, fun, and entertaining.
2. Most of Rowena's stories are about young, smart pigs.
3. Rowena was once a young pig herself, but now she is almost grown up.
4. Each night, Rowena tells a different story.
5. Squirmy, a young worm, loves to listen to stories.
(Parentheses indicate deletions)
6. How can one pig, all by herself, tell all those(,) stories?
7. On Halloween, Rowena(,) tells spooky stories.
8. One especially spooky story, *Ghost Pig*, is about a spooky pig.

Grammar & Gramps (page 38)
You Answer It!: Havent, Im, Theyr'e, you're, Theyr'e, Ill, dont, Im, Ill
1. hasn't
2. wasn't
3. didn't
4. they're
5. haven't

The Lost Balloon (page 39)
You Answer It!: horse's
1. Judy's
2. Woovis's or Woovis'
3. kit's
4. Monica's
5. friends'
6. weeks'
7. people's
8. audience's
9. explorers'
10. balloon's
11. adventurers'

Street Smarts (page 40)
You Answer It!: it's / its
1. Squirmy's
2. hers
3. mine
4. yours
5. colony's
6. people's
7. ours

Live at Ha-Ha's (page 41)
You Answer It!: "Why do you want us to trample your potato crop?" The farmer says, "I'm trying to grow MASHED potatoes."
1. "Welcome to the Ha-Ha Comedy Club," Woovis said.
2. "Tonight I'll be telling you some of my finest jokes," added Woovis.
3. A skunk in the audience asked, "Can you tell some jokes about skunks?"
4. Woovis said, "Hmm. I know one skunk joke, but it's a real stinker."
5. "Tell it anyway," said the skunk. "I love skunk jokes."
6. The mouse said, "Excuse me but I'd like to hear some mouse jokes."
7. "Mouse jokes aren't funny," said the alligator. "I'd rather hear gator jokes."
8. "Alligator jokes stink!" cried the skunk. "Can't you tell more skunk jokes?"

Wooden Shoe (page 42)
You Answer It!: "Tell me more Knock Knock jokes."
1. Squirmy asked Woovis, "Can we interview you for *Weekly Blab* magazine?"

2. "Sure," Woovis said, "that sounds like a great idea."
3. "How does it feel to be a famous comedian?" Squirmy inquired.
4. "I'm not all that famous," Woovis said. "I've never been on TV."
5. Molly added, "I've heard that the networks want to give you your own show."
6. "It's possible," Woovis replied. "I'm not sure I'm ready for my own show."

Oh Iowa! (page 43)
You Answer It!: Its (*It's*); your (*you're*); Lets (*Let's*)
1. its
2. Your
3. their
4. its
5. It's

Review Section 3 (page 44)
(Parentheses indicate deletions)
1. Woovis' (his) rock and roll band was not good at singing, playing, or dancing.
2. On March 30, 2000, Woovis dissolved the band.
3. At that point, Woovis had no job, no money, and no car.
4. So, Woovis went to Hollywood, California, to see his friend Rowena.
5. Rowena's job was to read movie script(')s.
6. "We're looking for good scripts about dogs," Rowena said.
7. "Hey, I'm a dog!" Woovis cried.
8. Woovis said, "You're looking at your next big screenwriter."
9. For three(,) months, Woovis worked feverishly on his script.
10. "It's the story of a dog who is handsome, smart, and talented," Woovis said.
11. "By any chance, could that dog be you?" Rowena asked.
12. "Don't be ridiculous!" Woovis said.
13. By August 5, 2000, the dog's script was finished.
14. Rowena gave it to a big movie director named Lefty Lewis.
15. "In my opinion it's really a lousy script," Lefty said.
16. Rowena tried other readers, but they felt the same way.
17. "You(')r(e) script is no good," Rowena told Woovis.
18. "Oh well! Back to the drawing board," Woovis said.

Woovis' Poetry Corner (page 46)
You Answer It!: present
1. past
2. present perfect
3. present
4. present
5. past
6. present progressive
7. present
8. future

Modern Art (page 47)
You Answer It!: I *have* seen it.
1. painted
2. sold
3. hoped
4. gotten
5. went
6. spoke
7. told

Superstition (page 48)
You Answer It!: I never *have been* superstitious.
1. has
2. has
3. has
4. hadn't
5. will have
6. (have) had
7. (had) have
8. (had) has

Liars and Layers (page 49)

You Answer It!: Moovis means cows never lie (always tell the truth), but Squirmy thinks she means cows never lie down (never recline).

1.	lie	2.	lay
3.	laid	4.	lay
5.	Lying, lying	6.	laid

Cold Spell (page 50)

You Answer It!: Come in out of the cold and *sit* down.

1.	sat	2.	set
3.	raised	4.	sitting.
5.	rose	6.	set

Review Section 4 (page 51)

1.	present	2.	progressive
3.	past	4.	progressive
5.	past perfect	6.	future perfect
7.	sit	8.	rose
9.	told	10.	gone
11.	gotten	12.	spoke

The Sea Biscuit (page 54)

You Answer It!: best, better

1.	best	2.	nicer
3.	terrible	4.	more
5.	faster	6	faster
7	ugliest		

Student Driver (page 55)

You Answer It!: I don't got no idea.

1.	most skillful	2.	any
3.	harder	4.	any
5.	easiest	6.	ever
7.	faster	8.	could

Homemade Donuts (page 56)

You Answer It!: You cook good. (well)

1.	good	2.	well
3.	well	4.	well
5.	good	6.	well
7.	well		

The Mighty Ant (page 57)

You Answer It!: wait /weight; ways/weighs

1.	ways	2.	except
3.	led	4.	past
5.	piece	6.	effect
7.	hear	8.	lead

The Matterpal (page 58)

You Answer It!: I only found one mistake on page 14. You included a word...

1. The title of Monica's storybook is *Bearly Tales*.
2. The book is about a bear named Monica.
3. In the book, Monica roams through the forest searching for honey.
4. She climbs up an oak tree and gets stuck between two branches.
5. "Help!" Monica shouts, but no one can hear her.
6. Monica gets stuck in the tree. Since she is stuck, she decides to eat the honey.
7. *She is* stuck in the tree for several hours without anyone in sight.

Job Interview (page 59)

You Answer It!: Let; The; The mail carrier dropped her mail bag in the river.

(Parentheses indicate deletions. Italics indicate spelling corrections.)

My New Job by Judy the Frog, Editor

I was hired by Rowena on May 5, 1999. What a day that was! Rowena put me to work right away. My first job *was* to edit a book about pigs, called THE WONDERFUL, WONDERFUL PIG. (Ill tell ya) I was really scared at first because I knew nothing about pigs! *However*, I learned *a lot* from editing the book. For *example*, did you know that pigs are one of the most *intelligent* animals? (They really are.) It took three weeks to edit the book. I learned a lot about pigs. I also learned many important editing skills. I will use these skills to edit my next book. Its title is THE WONDERFUL, WONDERFUL FROG.

Review Section 5 (page 60)

1.	best	2.	any
3.	well	4.	accept
5.	strangest	6.	good
7.	led		

8. Suddenly, we realized that the book was(,) a hit.
9. Woovis became a star. He was mobbed wherever he went.
10. After dozens of Woovis books, movies, and TV appearances, *Woovis became* the world's number-one celebrity dog.